Faith Through Poetry

God's Will

(Inspired by St. Mark Baptist Church of Flint, MI)

By Terralisa McBride

Prologue

Being the daughter of alcoholics, introduced me to a whole new world of lies, lust, deceit, and mental anguish. However, I have found a new way to live my life as I approached my adult years. Although, my up bringing is still imprinted in my mind, the fact remains that I have become my own woman. I still think of the days when my mother and father were still alive and how much I still wish they could just scold me one more time.

I am learning to accept my wrongs because they teach me to be right. I have loved, lost, played the field, and been played. I know that my life is not peaches and cream, it's more like cereal without milk or macaroni without cheese. Everyone struggles, this is true, but it is up to that specific person to dictate how they engage their own situation. The following short stories and poems are all driven from true life events of mine and of those who are in my surroundings. Some of the things I talk about may hit home with you or make you wonder if the stories or poems I'm speaking of is about you. As the saying goes "if the shoe fits wear it". My life adventures, trials, and tribulations have affected the way I live my life.

Each of us has our own destiny and somehow, we are all connected to each other. As I've said before I truly believe that this is my gift from GOD, to have the ability to bring life to words on paper and touch the depth of any one person. I hope you find interest in my work and continue to follow my writings as I take this leap into a whole new world of the life as a licensed author, writer, & poet.

Dedication

With all of my heart, this book is dedicated to Ja'Nyah, Jabri, Jene', Jayden, and Jhy'Lah. These little people will soon grow up to be my biggest support. I love the love that they give me, GiGi, as I am known to them. I also want to acknowledge my Pastor Kevin Thompson for believing in me and my work and for allowing me to display my talent in his sanctuary. I also want to acknowledge Elder Agnes Naphier my second mom that God has gifted to my life. Last but not least, I dedicate this book of uplifting words to my only daughter Jeree and my only son Eugene II. I hope that my life experiences give you both inside knowledge of how God is essential in everyday life and how He delivered me.
I love you all and my words of wisdom, peace, and joy cover you all of your days around the sun.

Amen!

The Love of A Mother

You start out as a gift and a blessing to the woman that carry's you in her womb. If you honor and respect her this same love is in, you all the way to your tomb. But do you realize that God made it so, Jesus Christ was a blessing to Mary and that is something you all should know.

The love of a mother is so sweet and so good. She has a heart big enough to spread through the neighborhood. The love that a true woman of God displays will give others hope for a brighter day. Our lord goo has a mysterious way of giving you back loved ones lost long ago, especially when you kneel and pray.

When you see a woman of faith you should want to touch her and gaze upon her face and receive the love that she has to show. You see the love you thought you lost or the loving feeling you want and that was missing is right before your eyes, listen to me this i know.

When you cry, she cries, she sees what's missing on the inside. The love from a mother comes in many forms because God knows what you need. All you have to do is believe. Believe in his power, believe in his glory god heard my cry and this is my story.

I miss my mom and my grandmom the most but God gave me elder Naphier to mend my heart I can see those women I miss within her spark and now she is the woman that sees me as I grow into a work of art.

The love from a mother begins with God as the head of our life. I am learning this through her. From her trials and tribulations along with her sacrifice. That's why I have changed my ways and constantly pray. Because i am under construction but I am on my way. Hallelujah thank you Jesus for the many blessings you have bestowed upon me. If heaven was a highway, I would speed all the way to thee.

Thank you, Jesus!

Thank you, Jesus, for waking me up today. Even though last night I did not pray. I sometimes take your power for granted; I get in your way throughout the day, I know my mind is a little slanted.

Thank you, Jesus, for carrying me. Especially when I lose my faith and I cannot see; all the things you made possible for me. Any given day I move about aimlessly, searching for a purpose when I should believe in thee. You are the Almighty, the Alpha, the Omega. We need to Honor thy father he is our Lord and Savior.

Thank you, Jesus, for having mercy over my soul. I need to be more obedient and remember the writings on the scrolls. Thank you, Jesus, please keep working on me. You performed many miracles in galilee, for I am a sinner so lowly and meek. It is your grace that I seek.

Thank you, Jesus, for knowing my heart. Giving me peace so I do not fall apart. With your guidance, I know I will be fine. I will keep leaning on you to ease my mind. Luke 24 vs 45 - when you learn how to trust and give God the glory no man can contradict nor copy your story.

Thank you, Jesus, for allowing me to re-discover myself. To understand my worth before I, leave this earth. Thank you, Jesus, for all that i see in this world that surrounds me. The longer I am here I can be of witness to thee. Same as the people who seen Jesus walk across the sea of Galilee John 6 vs 19. I will not be afraid this is where I want to be, to hear your words, come follow me.

F.O.C.U.S

Find. Our. Christ. in U. Soon.
Focus on your own journey while you walk this land, keep in mind there is a greater plan. For you, for I, for this entire land. Putting all your faith in man will surely strike you where you stand. The devil moves quickly to get in you and grab you with his hands. Then it's hard to break free so I suggest you fall on bended knee. Pray out loud speak in tongues let the devil know he has not won.
F.O.C.U.S
Find. Our. Christ. in U. Soon.
Before the devil consumes you and brings you to your doom.

Lost Souls

When you meet someone, you approach them with respect. Your inner soul will open up when you try to connect. Some people you meet come with bad intentions their outer layers give you false hope of joy while your inner layers have apprehension.

As you engage in friendly conversations discerning this new person with stipulations has you wondering if it's worth the risk like deep sea diving for crustaceans.

Everyone has a soul, but some souls don't connect with the spirit. They walk the earth speaking out loud for everyone to hear it. But they have no discernment of the spirit.

Be wise, stay true, study God's word he is here for you. Pray unto him with convictions of your heart, allow yourself to be renewed & begin a fresh start. Remembering there are people who will build you up and also tear you apart, these people don't have souls they are creatures of the dark.

If you believe in our lord god you will feel him deep in your soul and no man, no woman can break your mold. We are created in his image inside & out he provide us with a soul to stand scream and shout, no doubt; but there are souls that people can control, misuse & abuse leave you left for dead or just simply confused.

If you were captured and taken to a different land, you lose your soul and you're not considered a man. If you were forced to work in unsafe conditions to become a handmaid, you lose your family ties & your ambitions.

Lost souls have no meaning, lost souls need spiritual healing. Where do you stand as a woman or a man? Are you a lost soul out of control? Gods unchanging hand can reset your mold.

Black

God has always been here. Even when the world was pitch black, God has always been here, even though we as his children fall back. Brought into a world unclear to most a spiritual war has been battling and all we see are ghost.
So, when we are here the angels bell ring know that we have always been kings and queens. God made the world we know, and it was here long before we were captured to be slaves and yet... We still mis-behave.
Tragedy came and swept us away made us do things against our will and-called us names. One thing we knew to hold onto is that God would come through, to give us strength & hope but some of us still hanged from a rope.
Our skin color has power that goes untold, so when you see your brothers & sisters let that love unfold. Cover them with black love power like the heavenly rain showers that covers the earth, something we should have been taught from birth. Noah's arch carried pairs of two and was big as a tower, when two or more are together you feel gods almighty love power.
There are many colors & nationalities of people god has embraced, this we know as the sun caress's our face; and yet some keep the black community in last place.
As we gather to praise God & sing spiritual hymns, we were still attacked & treated wrong just because our skin was black. God makes no mistakes, but some try to be him in their own twisted way. That's when we stand & fight... Power to the people say it with all your might!!!

The belt of truth, the breast plate of righteousness, the gospel of peace, the shield of faith, the helmet of salvation & the sword of the spirit. Sounds so good and true, especially, when God is in you.
Our history, our people, our kind should see how important it is to wear the amour of God as protection from Satan in this spiritual war before he attacks, because when your mind is dark there is no warm light it's just cold and black.

The Days of Our Lives

Today may be full of tears and sorrow, but tomorrow will be a mystery to follow. Last week was unexpected, last month you didn't know if you'd make it.
Every hour you have to think, every second your eyes blink. When the days of our lives starts the countdown of our days, your mind starts to wonder especially if you haven't prayed. When will it all end? Have I covered all my sins? What am I leaving behind? Did I even try to open my eyes? Has everyone I've loved or debated, gave me back the same love and not hesitated?
The days of our lives God has created it to be. God also knows when the end is to be. Even if we don't see or believe it to be. The almighty has all power so be careful of the day and the hour. You'll never know what lies ahead, you can exist no more and have never left your bed.
This afternoon may bring you joy. This evening may make you laugh, but the journey you follow could easily be your last. The days of our lives comes with an expiration. Stay prayed up and have high expectations.
Today may be full of sorrow & tears, but our lord has an unchanging hand that can heal. With his love, you will feel safe, he has a home in a heavenly place. The days of our lives can sweep you off your feet, the winds of time can blow on a different beat. Live your life to the fullest and keep God in it. The days of our lives can close doors and darken your path with you consumed in it.

Philippians 4:13

I can do all things through Christ who strengthens me.
4:13

4:13 is not just a number or the time, 4:13 will put something deep on your mind. Four is an angel number to remind you that you are safe. Thirteen is a sacred number to bring good luck and prosperity to those who embrace.

There is a notion that devotion is for every child of god, not just Christians as it is mentioned, but for sinners like you & me, trying to get gods attention. God so loved the world he gave his only son. Believe in him and your battle shall be won.

He never said that the struggle is not real, or your earthly problems will be fixed, taken away, or healed. As long as you have faith no trial or tragedy is too hard to face. 4:13 not just a number or a place; 4:13 is truly God's good grace.

Remember what four means, also thirteen, the good days, the bad days, & the grey days in between. Keep leaning on our lord and Savior and you'll find Favor. Come unto God many have followed, lay your burden down & be grateful for tomorrow.

When the clock strikes 4:13 you are aware of the time whether its am or pm you should seek the divine. 4:13 not just a number or the time 4:13 will put something deep on your mind.

Amen.

Philippians 4:13
I can do all things through Christ who strengthens me.

Praise God (Keeping) Business as Usual

Man is tested with a message, yet God knows all. God gives man a good heart but it's his woman that sometimes makes him fall. Pray to our father lock your soul within. Come unto Jesus Christ, he can save us all; even when we sin. It is written on the walls and the scrolls you've seen, so believeth in thee; God who created the human being. He sacrificed his only son because he loves you and me.

Some people the devil has won and that you can clearly see. We walk this earth amongst all kinds some of us astray and follow the blind. It doesn't matter if you're a woman or a man we are all his children reaching for his hand. With all the misery and pain in this world nobody can stand praise god amen.

Honor thy father he has a plan. Come unto him, conduct your business as usual, living to be focused and free of sin. Defeat Satan keep him beneath your feet please don't let him in. When the devil shows up in many forms, he could look like you or me. But if we keep walking our own path to glory keeping our faith, and doing God's work, the devil has no power so stump him in the dirt.

Praise God keeping business as usual.

Pieces of me

Have you ever fell apart? Can you glue an open wound? How many slaps can you withstand? Are you a woman or a man? When can you begin to feel whole? How can one be so bold? Inside becomes outside and yet you still bend! Is this your lover or your friend?

Can you see all the parts of you that leak? Why does the heart make you so weak? Do you think your life is just? Is there anyone you can trust? Have you ever given your all just to see yourself fall? Did you learn a lesson or is this a blessing?

When you open up, do you expose the real you? Can you honestly speak truth on the life you live? Or is this all smoke and mirrors just a fib? Why does a person string you along? Sometimes even playing your favorite song!

Pieces of me are all over the place. But you seem to be the one to put a smile on my face. If you can pull in all the hurt and find the right things to say. You have found all the pieces of me and i could love on you every single day.

Knowledge is Power

As I lie awake and breathe God has my attention, when I pray, I hear him speak. As my faith gets strong, I know I won't go wrong, even when my words are weary, I'll just sing a song. Sometimes my soul is weak, that's why on my knees I pray to learn and seek, the knowledge of our Lord and Savior. Thank you, father, for all my woe's I know your presence has gone untold. I've learned to change my behavior because life is worth living even when we cannot stand, I am learning to hold on to God's unchanging hand. When I say living, I am not speaking upon this earth, dwelling in God's mansion that has many rooms, when it's time for you to rest, he will have a bed for you. Thank you, father, I believe in you through and through, your knowledge is power I will keep my faith in you.

A Child of God

Dear mom and dad, thank you for giving me life, for teaching me things and bringing me up right. I am your child; God gave me to you. I am very thankful this is true. Because both of you are God's children too.

I love the lord I see in you. As I learn to serve the lord it feels good because our home is on one accord. Giving Honor to God the head of our life, loving each other and learning more about Jesus Christ.

A child of God comes in many forms. When you are baptized you are re-born. No weapon formed against us shall prosper. Dad and mom, I would love you even if you were fosters. The lord protects our family, this is what i have learned to see. I am a child of God this is who I claim to be.

Dear mom and dad. Keep bringing me to church so as I row older, I can teach my children how to serve our God First. Magnify and praise his holy name, I am a child of God let's continue to pray.

Amen!

When The Lord Wakes Me Up

As the seasons change each day is new. So, say your prayers at night before the mornings dew. Give thanks to God for waking you. Every night the world has a different story. Be thankful for everything you have but give God the glory.

When the lord wakes me up all I want is to hold his hand, even when I cannot see him stand up like a man. I believe in his power, I praise his holy name, every day the lord wakes me up I have blood running through my veins. My heart is warm and has a beat, my soul and my spirit are solid as I stand on two feet.

When the lord wakes me up, I want to have purpose driven joy, with a big smile on my face. Because I have another chance to love him and receive his grace. Lord have mercy on me, there are lot of things I have to go through each day. Which makes me want to kneel and pray. But without you near I would live in fear, so every day the lord wakes me up my mind is clear.

I have a reason to be here, to mentor to others who need some spiritual healing. If you love the lord that feeling is thrilling. When the lord wakes me up the first thing, I do is say thank you God for waking me up. Because of you father god I have Favor. I praise your holy name you are my lord and Savior.

Amen!!!

Smile

For every encouraging smile there is an encouraging moment. It shows support to positively uplift anyone who catches it. As it is an act of atonement. Just like when little children were brought to Jesus, he filled them with love and hope. He smiled to show them they were safe in his presence with some comforting words they could quote. A smile comes from the heart so deep within, give your life to God no need to live in sin.

Smile as often as you can. Do not put all your faith in one woman or man. Bring joy to the world it is a part of god's plan. He is the one man that truly understands. Smile in the mirror give yourself a fresh start every day. Just also remember to kneel and pray and praise his holy name. A smile can change your mood, it can open your thoughts, it can also make someone forget their faults.

It is so easy to show the god in you, with just a simple smile. Don't you know he loves us unconditionally in spite of our wrongs or lifestyles. God is good, God is great, Jesus wept for our sins and our mistakes. I suggest you practice what he preached, you still have time to be lowly and meek. Have compassion and be humble Noah had an arch it was not a jungle.

Smile at one another give God the praise. Love thy neighbor is not a metaphoric phrase. It is the teachings of our lord and Savior hallowed be thy name. Smile more, frown less, live in the word Honor his message and be blessed.

The Voice of Reason

Shhhh!!!!
Did you hear?

I think you were talking in your head and your thoughts are not very clear. When you are alone your mind begins to wonder your thoughts and your reality start to feel like the sound of thunder.

My lord is listening to you talk with in your mind. You say all kinds of things, but you are wasting a lot of time. If you listen to the voice of reason, you will have peace and sit still. Because if you believe in our god then surely you know that he is real. You need to lean on him, walk with him, hold on to his hand and become that righteous woman or man.

The voice of reason will enter your thoughts even if you have several faults. This voice is like no other tone it feels you up when you are rested and alone. The voice of reason is very powerful it does have meaning just like this world changes seasons.

When God grasp's your attention you should be humble and listen. Peace be still as I had mentioned. We are all under construction and some foundations are shaky, because we do not pray and pay attention even when our life is breaking.

Shhhh!!!!
Did you hear?

The voice of reason is very loud and clear. Amen!

The Moment You've Been Waiting For

How do you know if you are blessed? Have you studied the word or are you waiting on the test. Do you have any feelings when you pray? Have you thanked God for waking you up today.

The moment you've been waiting for never come, but you are a witness that miracles can happen for some. Your understanding of God may not be what others think. However, you can be gone today or tomorrow in just one blink.

The moment you've been waiting for might arise, then here is your daily issues...surprise!! Now you're screaming out God to fix your life and help you unfold. Because you thought you had it all under control.

The moment you've been waiting for is right now, kneel and pray get to know God somehow. Don't let the moment you've been waiting for vanish and disappear. God said come unto me have no fear. I am the way the truth and the light. Bare your soul to me, it will be alright, surrender and repent please do not resent my omnipotence.

I am the moment you've been waiting for. I am your present your future and your past, believe in me even if you cannot see me while looking through broken glass.

Steps

Moving right along grooving to a new beat jumping, skipping around, running, and taking all kinds of leaps. Not paying attention nor watching your steps. Praising money till you have nothing left.

Steps are your calculated moves, some steps go up, some steps go down and some steps you take will put you in the ground. If you were measured by every step you take. You should caution yourself and take a leap of faith.

This step is not measured by link chains on a football field. It is measured by discernment and faith because God is real. If you move this link chain an inch in the right direction, it may not be much, but it will feel like perfection.

The more you proclaim our Lord and Savior, you will be blessed and highly favored. Steps you take even if you backslide can be better steps with God by your side. Don't take steps too fast or too slow, allow yourself the room to blossom and grow.

Step into a new life with God. Hallelujah praises his holy name step on the enemy, tap dance on his head. Keep him beneath you because he wants you dead. Different steps can alter your groove, keep stepping with God and you will see how much he loves you.

Amen

Stepping Into Blessings Walking Out on Faith

Do you agree that we have 2 feet, 2 hands, 2 eyes, 2 ears, 2 legs, and 2?
Arms. Attached to 1 body, 1 heart, 1 soul, 1 nose, 1 mouth and 1 life. Have you given thought that our lord collectively designed you and I to endure all things in our path with many mountains to move.

These 12 parts above will make you whole, but you will never know the true meaning without God, I am not trying to be bold. Because stepping into blessings means you are using the tools that God has allowed you to function with. Also walking out on faith with the discernment of the spirit will keep you focused on your goals god set forth for you to get.

Did you know that the 12 apostles that continued to deliver the teachings of Jesus after his crucifixion, went everywhere to preach his word, it was Jesus' decision. They utilized the tools god gave them to roam the land walking out on faith under the leadership of one man. Did you know that the 12 apostles were baptized and already stepping into blessings. Each of them was a part of the foundation of the church to spread the gospel all over the earth.

You should believe in his power and praise his holy name. Start stepping into blessings and walking out on faith. Teach everyone you know about our lord above show them how Jesus Christ is love. Today you should walk out on faith and step into your blessings give Honor to God. Start caressing and confessing, your 1 life with gods will. To do good even when you feel ill. Stepping into blessings and walking out on faith is God's love and it cannot be replaced.

Amen!!!

Walking With Faith Between the Raindrops

When the storm arises, and the sun hides behind the clouds.
The rain forms to penetrate and nourish the ground in which
we all must be laid down. Walking with faith is what you
should learn to do. Staying dry between the raindrops means
God is covering you.

His grace and his mercy have weight, please do not ignore
and for the love of God keep your faith. When moments in
time break you down you tend to rewind the events that got
you this way. Sometimes the soul is ugly but has a pretty face,
this is when you truly need God's favor to live in this unruly
place. Scurrying around picking up pieces from the ground.
Unaware that you are wearing a frown and moving around
like a clown with grief on your face.

You should be honorable and true because this will show the
god in you. The saying goes when it rains it pours, please
understand this world is not yours. You are a specimen made
of many molecules God created. He has many plans for you,
the Bible has stated it. So let no one man or woman make
you stop. Because walking between the raindrops in the mist
of your storm is a blessing that holds you and keeps you nice
and warm. When mental issues of life cause you to just stop.
Talk to God, hold your head up high and walk with faith
between the raindrops.

Amen!!!

The Light

In the dark there is no light to be seen, that's when your vision is clear if you have faith and believe. Believe that God said let there be light to help guide you on your way. You can see beyond the horizon; he just wants you to pray. Praising God is such a joyful noise that your inner being has no null and void. You should open your mind and fill your heart. Because without the light of God you would just be living in the dark.

Jesus said I am the way to my father your one true king. He is responsible for all created living things. The light is the source, but of course the dark side of things will show you a different image of you, the devil will corrupt your life, with a blow that stings. Because the devil is responsible for all nasty things. You do know that things move at night. Especially when you have no sight, no power, and no prayer. You can roam this land and yet be stagnant holding the enemy's hand. When you entertain the king of darkness, you're giving him his due. This is not the plan God has set for you.

The darkness brings out another life you begin to live. You learn new ways to satisfy the enemy because you refuse to pray you rather sin. But our Lord is always there by your side watching you run astray. Waiting patiently for you to yell out his name, kneel and pray. God gives us light within our soul. This light will illuminate you to shine bright as gold. Your faith and your praise are all you need, to have God help you defeat the enemy. Give Honor to God and keep him in sight, stop living in the dark keep your faith and let God turn on the light

God's Army

We may be young with limited site. We are a part of God's army with a strong will to fight.

Not with words or weapons to be clear. We will use Jesus Christ our Savior so have no fear.

God is mighty, God is just, he created the heavens and the earth so that we can rise from ashes, dirt, and dust.

Our faith grows stronger as we continue to pray. His eye is on the sparrow as we praise his holy name.

In God's army is where we want to be. Covered with the blood of Jesus, this battle is not about you and me.

We are equipped and protected; Hallelujah thank you Jesus we are doing what is expected.

Amen!

Mind*Heart*Flesh

Your mind? Your heart? Or your flesh?

Which one enables you and puts you to the test! Because when you fail you cannot easily rest.

-Your mind is a strong powerful tool it can cause you to run around acting a fool. Or pretend to be in control when it's not true. No one see's the god in you.

-Your heart is a weapon without the proper nourishments it can cause you to kill or be killed. Take this message as a lesson.

-Your flesh lusts against the spirit- Galatians 5:16-17 read it to adhere it. This is a war that starts within, believe in our lord please do not commit a sin.

Gods most precious gift is when he created man equipped with a mind, a heart, and flesh to walk on land and to be his best. As we are created in his image it is God's plan for us to walk in the spirit. You need to read the word and understand how-to live-in it. He believes in you; He just wants you to be committed.

When your mind defeats you and your heart becomes hard your flesh will get weak and now satin is in charge. Your mind is no longer strong, your heart is no longer a weapon, your flesh will lust with most while your spirit is now a ghost.

Fill your mind with god's words, open your heart and observe. Believe in your spirit and behave with your flesh. Protect your soul with the armor of God open your mouth and confess. Before satin has you bound with a messy mind. No heart and weak flesh. He will destroy any and all things that God loves the Best.

After All

Do you know where you came from?
Do you know why you are here?

Have you given this life any thought? Has God's message
been clear? what will you stand up for who will be there when
you fall? Does God's love matter to you after all? Or just
when you need a favor before you crash and burn - is that the
only time you fall to your knees and pray for his grace?
Something you didn't earn after all.

You never know what the day will bring, and you pretend to
love thee almighty king. he brings joy to your heart when you
hear church bells ring. After all is said and done who do you
lean on? where do you turn? have you given God any praise
because his love. Has to be earned.

He shows you mercy - that's when you stand proud and tall,
but you never read your bible so how will you learn anything
after all?
When closed doors get opened it's something to be said
about that notion. It's called the word of God so, give
devotion.

With God no issue is too big or small. give honor to the one
that spares you every day of your life. because He is always
there after all.

Amen!!!

Follow the Leader

As you wake up every morning and perform the same task. How long will you do this? Or better yet, how long will it last? Repetition pulls us in, just as we were born in the iniquity of sin. The devil wants to destroy you and alter the victory you seek within.

Follow the leader everyone wants to follow. Stop following everyone who seeks a new leader today and/ or tomorrow. When your calling allows you to serve 10 years as a blessed humble servant; the words you speak touch deep. They have a strong hold because God gave you the credentials to be told.

We at St. Mark Baptist Church of Flint, honor our pastor Kevin Thompson, the loyal servant is he. We learn how to pray and serve thee Almighty Father God and pray on bended knee. You do know that pastors are the vessel to the light. To God be the glory we should pray every day and every night, that our pastor continues to motivate and teach us about our father god, the leader to follow.

Pastor Thompson, we love you today and every day after tomorrow. Thank you! For being an obedient servant, for your dedication, support, and love. So, I am asking, who will you choose to be the head of your life? What have you offered, given, or sacrificed? The god we serve can change your life, the pastor you follow needs a vision so bright, that you can see the lord in plain sight.

Find a pastor that stands strong and true, pastor Kevin Thompson for the next 10 years plus!!! We are here with you.

Motivation vs. Temptation

When life looks promising, you believe you are at your best.
When you have faith and praise the Lord, there is now a test.

Temptation has you believing what you see is true and yet
motivation is only witnessed by a few.

When God pulls you through, you are excited and mark off a
check on your prop list. When you forget to praise him daily
then you wonder why you're not accomplished.

Motivation for Christ should be all you need to feel his love.
Temptation looking for love will never be as beautiful as a
snow-white dove.

Give honor to God, he can motivate you and that you can
trust, because temptation is a sign of weakness, and it happens
to all of us.

Be tempted by God my fellow brothers and sisters in Christ.
Let the lord lead you and be the head of your life. Let God
motivate you and give you power. We need him to defeat the
enemy every hour.

Are you moved by motivation or tempted by temptation?
Lord god I pray you heal our nation.

The Battle

Open your heart, close your eyes, hold your tongue give it to God and your battle is won. It is not yours to fight, the devil is real even if not in site. Open your ears, extend your arms, love thy neighbor give plenty of hugs that's no harm. The world we live in has many depts of hell to say the least.

We dwell amongst snakes also known as the belly of the beast. It has been said that the serpent could speak and move about like humans but not on the same beat. His deceiving ways had him cursed and forever to crawl on his belly and eat dirt. -

If an apple a day keeps the doctor away, then keeping your faith can keep the devil away. With out your belief in God, the devil's playground is in your path. You need to be prepared for a wicked blood bath. He is not your friend, he is not powerful, but he has a way to keep you doubtful.

This battle began long ago, before you were conceived in the womb and given life to grow. You are connected to your mother's navel this is your life force because God made this able. When something is wrong, your mother can feel this deep within. Just like God can so stop trying to resist him and live in sin.

God's power is holy, God's power is divine this battle will go on until the end of time. Always know God has the last say so, and who's report is you going to believe. Whose side are you on? How will you fight? When you are not covered with the armor of God who should be the head of your life. When will you stop running and start praying on your knees? Because if this battle consumes you, i am certain you will pray to God for mercy. Amen!!

Forgiveness

Before I go to sleep and when I wake up, I say a prayer, but throughout the day I want to swear. Forgive me lord I am not perfect in anyway, but I will serve you until the end of my days. At the feet of Jesus is where I need to be, forgive me lord because some days I cannot see. All the things you have allowed me to do that keeps me here, forgive me lord because it is you that, I fear.

Forgiveness is what I seek, I pray to the lord my soul to keep. Continue having authority over this human vessel, my lord and Savior you are my perfect pedestal. I admire your greatness, I magnify your name, Jesus Christ was nailed to the cross for my sins and my shame.

Forgive me lord for my stagnant unjust ways. I have been tainted by man and yet I am   still to blame. You made it clear, and you showed me how. To leave it with you and lay my burdens down. Isaiah 41:10 plays a melody in my mind as I imagine walking bare feet in the sand. God says he will uphold me with his righteous right hand.

Forgiveness my lord is what I want to show. It is you father god I want to get to know. With you I have hope because I cannot do it on my own. I know I will reap what I sow, please work on my spirit so that my anointing will continue to grow.

The Calling

I am who God called me to be I stand beside pastors, elders, & deacons that will teach me about thee. He is almighty, He is just, God puts us where we need to be so that we can thrive and thrust. This is our family we pray for one another. From babies to teens and all in between. So, bring your father and your mother. We welcome you all, give Honor to God, he will catch you when you fall.

When you look around, we have many who play a part in this church. The nurses and ushers all display their heart, no need to go far, no need to search, because these people are right here at St. Mark Baptist Church. Giving us support and love come join us as we send praises above. When you give yourself to our lord, your voice is heard, and you can get filled up on the word.

When you welcome the calling, know that it's just for you, because you matter on this earth and God's love is true. It's an honor and it will give you peace, when God calls on you this is a joy you can release. Some have stopped believing in his power and glory. I say look at us & let us tell our story. God makes no mistakes, and the calling is real. This is our choice as we learn from you, others will hear our voice.

Amen

When You Give the Devil His Due!!

When you give the devil his due, He attacks you and your crew, but what do you do when the crew abandons you?

When you do the devil's deed. He has a way of keeping you from falling to your knees. He will show you all that glimmers and glows until he delivers that deadly blow.

But "God" said I have all power; you have allowed Satan to entertain you and make you sour. My child the devil was an angel cast down from above because of his ways. He wants to destroy you, but I will show you love the godly way.

Satan is not powerful he is in your mind. Something you cannot escape from time after time. If you give me your profound faith, I'll keep you safe, because when you give the devil his due, he will keep you locked up in his place.

His place is not above or beneath. His place is deep in the center of the earth, beyond heavens peaks. Come unto me I'll give you free will before the devil has his due, that will cause you to murder & kill.

I'm not talking about a person or mankind. He will kill your most precious gift. I'm talking about he will kill your mind. When you give the devil, his due it is hard for you to escape. Have faith in me I'll carry you through and keep you safe.

Amen

The Stranger Within

When was the last time you smiled? Because I always see you cry, not with tears I can hear it when you sigh!!

Who do you talk to when times are tough? Have you called out to God or is that too much? The battle is not yours please try to understand. He moves and talks, you may not see him walk but I assure you, he is a real spiritual, godly man.

Have you ever encountered a person you really did not know? But yet you shared something personal about yourself this stranger would never have known. And somehow you call on God when times are rough, your plea the blood of Jesus to cover your mistakes & lift you up.

But when God speaks to you, his power is overlooked, and you ignore all the signs because you now say the victory is mines. God giveth and God taketh away - you give your faith to man, and you never pray.

However, He will never leave you, he will be there till the end. He knows you better than any friend. You just don't know yourself you lie, and you sin. You are moving too fast wanting to win. You are a child of God but also you are the stranger with in.

Joys Of the Soul

Happy feelings bring out beautiful smiles. A nice warm hug will carry you many miles. Every organ inside of you makes this wonderful concoction that God brewed, it's called an individual real-life stew.

We all have the same ingredients, but some stews have more seasons, I'll tell you why, here is the reason. It's called joys of the soul a Jesus Christ ingredient. I'll invite you to dinner, but this dinner you cannot eat.

However, you will get full and it's a wonderful, delightful, treat. It's called the word, and it is a powerful, strong grip that will make you move your feet. This Sunday dinner mmmm it cannot be beat.

Happy feelings bring out beautiful smiles. Giving Honor to God is worth the while. Hallelujah, thank you lord for this tantalizing fulfillment of my vibe. Joys of the soul, open up your bible and give this meal a try.

When God Found Me

I knew where I was going, but I felt lost. Keeping my hopes up and my fingers crossed. I didn't know what to say but my heart was not filled, and I did not know how to pray, and I could not sit still. Many people have tried to analyze and assist. But somehow my mind continued to resist.

One day I thought I had it together. Things seemed okay, but even when I thought of God I still did not pray. Once I decided to make a change, to visit a place where the church bells rang. My inner thoughts took over and once again the life I live was still full of sin & in disorder.

I will not and did not give up on myself I am a prized token, even when everything around me seemed to be broken. Where can i go for a peace of mind before this life of mines runs out of time.

When God found me, I was at my low. He spoke to me and said my child lets go. I knew what I had to do and follow my truths, you see the person I have been running away from was me it wasn't you. My mind was made up and my soul felt free, I closed my eyes and counted - 1. 2. 3.

When God found me, I discovered my true self, I no longer need to hide or feel lost because Jesus Christ died to pay the cost. The cost for me to live just & free when God found me, he held me with his loving hands and give me a reason to be.

When God found me, I now have a plan. A plan to praise and rejoice in his holy name. Give yourself away and let God find you so that you can do the same.

Amen!!!

Water

Before anyone was aware of land, all that could be seen is a body of water. Before life begins, it is also surrounded by a body of water. Each organ in our body has a level of water it holds. God made sure we are flourished with water to fill our souls. Water can take on different forms. It can be liquid or solid and even come out of your pores.

A bottle of water is like a human soul, it has an outer layer but not of skin and bone. It can be half full or half empty, so if God is not in your life - for you, I have sympathy. Reason is, once you remove the cap off the bottle, the water will evaporate. If you do not put a cap on your life with God, your soul already has an expiration date.

Water is an essential element. It is a part of everything, from paper to dirt and dust. All the reason in God we trust. He made us in the like of his image; he breathed breath into our nostrils and gave us life, he also ultimately gave his only son as sacrifice. When Jesus turned water into wine it represents the holy spirt, sacrifice and wisdom.

When you want to be renewed through Christ, the church will perform a baptism. This represents the death and resurrection of our lord and Savior, praise our god to receive his favor. Water is important to the body and soul. Don't dry out before you grow old. Open up your cap and refill your inner being, Jesus is the way from what I am seeing. You could be a woman or a man, place your body in God's un-changing hand. Drink from the fountain of life. Jesus Christ performed many miracles so teach our youth, let them know the bible has the proof.

Amen!!!

"Mission Impossible"

When it's quiet your mind drifts away, your body stands still while your thoughts run wild, but is your heart fulfilled? Or is it meek and mild.

When your faults become reality and your truths are lies, everyone can see you living this disguise. Can you deal with the facts or is this all acts. Do you have intentions or is this your mission.

You can't fool God even when you pretend, he is the Alpha and Omega he sees all our sins. It is impossible to look yourself in the face unless it's in a mirror and that image cannot be replaced. Who are you? Who do you want to be? God ask for nothing; his salvation is free.

If you believe in him whole heartedly and true, he gives you peace and He'll have a place for you to rest too. They say Jesus comes like a thief in the night. But do you really understand that's when he makes it alright?

Mission impossible is a message to be noted. A child of God can speak and truly be quoted. Especially if you study and read the word, God speaks loudly you just haven't heard, mission impossible where do you stand? Take a deep breath, think about it....

Amen!!!

For the Love of God!!!

For the love of God -what would you do? For the love of God - How far would you go?
For the love of God - you will reap what you sow!

God has love for you - but what if he didn't believe in you? God has love for you - but what if he let you fail and fall in a trap? God has love for you - but you do not have time to love him back!!

For the love of God - why do you forsake him?
For the love of God -why do you avoid peace and rest?
For the love of God- many have succeeded and been blessed!!!

God has love for you - his grace is like a shower. God has love for you - forever his love will grow.
God has love for you-believe in his power, this I know.

For the love of God - stand strong and pray with all your might! For the love of God - give yourself away and have some faith, he is alright for the love of God - live, love, honor, and praise His holy name!

God has love for you - but will you love him the same?

For the love of God - what's the matter? Who are you trying to blame?

God has love for you - can you comprehend and maintain?

For the love of God - don't let the devil win and drive you insane! God has love for you - don't let the sacrifice of his son be in vain!!!

Living In the Dash with Intentions:

Your time starts the moment you leave the womb. Your time ends the moment you are carried to your tomb.

Can you calculate the moments that lay in between? Would you do it all over again with all the things you have witnessed and seen?
What gets your gears moving? What will slow you down? Do you believe a smile can change your day or do you fuss, cuss and frown then bring all around you down?

Where is your joy? Is today a good day or will you be coy? Think about the beginning -think about the end unforeseen. What are you prepared to do in between; the first date and the last, what are your intentions while living in the dash? Moments of time do not move in reverse; you are tested by faith by an entity not of this universe.

Remember there is a space in between of our life with time. Live, laugh, love, and honor God remember Jesus turned water into wine. Have the audacity of hope, seriously this life is not a joke. Som times you have to rejoice and have great intentions. Have faith receive the word of God and start your own mission.

When family and friends walk away' from your tomb, our thoughts, and memories we speak hold true of you, right from the moment you left the womb. As we all are trying to understand life's intentions really fast; and wonder just how we will live out our own life in the dash.

You Should Appreciate the Servant of God

A vision, an incident, a word, a message these are a few things that come as a gift. They also can spiritually inspire one or uplift. Offering your services and to.be humble while you do a good deed. Pleases our lord the almighty king. You should appreciate the servant of God; they are the ones that die daily to sin and the fleshly desires as they suffer but will still put out the fires.

When you do things from your heart, please know that God is near. He walks beside his humble servants, so they do not live in fear. We all need to say, "lord God I am here, I come with my family to bond our beliefs this year". You should appreciate the servant of God even if you feel he or she is beneath your level.

You should never disrespect, ignore or treat them like a fool stop playing games we are not in school. Unless you are a rebel kicking them like a pebble while this same person will work beside you not afraid to use a shovel. Because in reality that makes you look suspicious and more like the devil.

You should appreciate the servant of God we are descendants of the meaning of Hebrew. If you know our Lord and you believe, he-bruised for you and I to be free. So that the world could see that sometimes the servant of God looks just like you or just like me. Open you mind be kind be made a new. Because how you react and respond you could be entertaining a servant of God this is true.

Peace Be Still

You can steal someone's joy; you can cause someone pain.
You can steal someone's hope and display all their shame.
But once you steal someone's peace you are going against
gods will. Job lost everything but he kept his faith in God
because he knew God is real.
You can enjoy your day; you can sit in peace. You need to
know that even though judas betrayed Jesus he still washed
his feet. He did this to all 12 of his disciples lovingly to show
he was humble, and a suffering servant of mankind. It also
displays the love we all have deep inside. John 13:1-8 will
explain, also it will teach you why you serve one another
without shame.
And yet you will worship people who carry iron steal, because
they act like they are in authority, and they give you a thrill.
But they will never show you any love or that they care.
Please understand that Jesus our lord and savior is
everywhere.
Satan is lurking to catch you and always busy on the job.
Then judas identified Jesus with a kiss for the lynch mob.
When you want peace and to be still follow God and you will.
Did you know he equipped Moses with skills to lead the
nation of Israel? Moses believed God to be real. Make no
mistake he proved it by turning his rod into a snake.
Abraham was willing to sacrifice his son for God. David
protected the sheep with his staff and his rod. Please know
you can protect your peace as well with the armor of God.

When you are troubled. Just say peace be still. You should learn to wait on God, He has all the answers for peace to be still. From the moon to the sun, the dark and the light. Follow the teachings of his plan to have his vision in sight. Peace be still, peace be still, no need to curse and fight. Love the lord. Find glory in his word. Peace be still I pray to the Lord that I am being heard.

I Am My Own Best Friend

I was given a beautiful name before I was born, but as I learned to speak and move about my name was torn. Torn into ugly words that I did not understand, like stupid, weirdo, retard and no one would shake my hand. I learned how to love from my father and mother, I have 2 little sisters I wish I had a brother.

As I grew older, I began a relationship with my toys, my computer, my pop it and my stick all brought me joy. Other kids my age would look and laugh some pushed me down and smashed my face in the grass. I got up and smiled because the person in me is not wild I am my own best friend I have my own style.

I am a little taller now and I've put on some weight, the next person that hurts me I still will not hate. I am my own best friend, I run free like sonic in the wind. The more I see how people treat me i don't understand why, I try my best not to cry.

Having a normal conversation, is what I thought I was doing; when I told my mom and dad that I've had enough of being sad. I want to be in a place that I cannot hear or see. I want to be in a place that I can rest easily. Keep a smile on my face and not be afraid of this un- worthy place.

I didn't realize that I made my mom cry I just wanted her to know that I am my own best friend until the day I die.

Blinded

Listen, hear, speak...
What is it that you seek?
If you can't see it, or touch it, do you believe if it's real? If you
feel it or smell it will that seal the deal!

God is unseen and yet he is always there. You feel his
embrace that can come out of nowhere.

Hear, speak, listen...
Do you know on the 3rd day he had arisen?
With out faith how do you live, do you wander this life with
nothing to give?

Will you give your life or a child as sacrifice? Remember he
did this for me and
You, be grateful, be true.

We may not see Him, but God sees you

Witness a Miracle

Witnessing a miracle means believing what you see, keeping your faith comes with a price that Jesus paid for you and me. The things they did to him, they did to you and me, they even hung us up beaten and bruised for the world to see. When God speaks the morning dew glistens, if your heart and mind is not developed nor focused; it's like little babies that don't listen.

Witnessing a miracle can change your life. Just like the women who touched Jesus' robe> Luke 8:43 - 48 now that's a story to be told. 12 years of hemorrhage she went broke looking for a cure. If seeing is believing this woman's heart had to be pure.

Witnessing a miracle is surprising and unexpected. Jesus died and rose up on the 3rd day his word and his message has come a long way. And yet some still don't detect it. Remember who you are and how you came to be. He died for our sins and still lives to set you free. All reasons why you should witness your miracle and pray on bended knee.

Witness Your Miracle.

He

He is she, whom has been credited from his rib. He is she, and now woman lives. Side by side from his side; God has spoken even when other temptations are around to hiss and poke. He is she that wondered off seeking more to tell. He is she listening to that judgement bell. He who has all power can only see the untold, he brought upon the light to a world unknown. It is He Lord God, the Alpha and Omega that loves us so. It is He Lord god that will show you that you will reap what you sow.

It is He that holds the key to set you free so you can win, it is he your salvation in spite of she that caused your sins. He brings glory in your heart, yet she can rip it up and tear it apart. With one little bite from a forbidden fruit, he is she whom destroyed your family roots. But when she disobeys, He, whom our Lord God choose to lead, it is she that fools He after God set him free. She that fools he does not want him to see. That when you lose touch with our lord and Savior you no longer represent, He.

He has to regain self-control; he has to know that some women will never show. That He was made from the divine, that he can last the test of time. When she, forgets the order of man. It is He our Lord God that will always stand, with an unchanging hand. Let he, know that he, Lord God is the man with the plan.

He

POWER IN PRAYER!!!

Giving our highest praise to the almighty king, does not cost a thing, so I say lift every voice & sing.
A LOT OF PRAYER A LOT OF POWER!!!
Understand that this battle in this world is not ours yet we take interest in the things without power. We spoil our riches & praise them until they are sour.
A LITTLE PRAYER A LITTLE POWER!!!
The devil comes to kill steal and destroy, and some people play with him as if he was a brand-new toy. Keep your faith in God and know that prayer is power because...
NO PRAYER NO POWER!!!
Read between the lines you just might receive this in your heart. I understood it the last time I visited St. Mark.

A LOT OF PRAYER A LOT OF POWER A LITTLE PRAYER A LITTLE POWER NO PRAYER NO POWER

Faith= forward all issues to heaven
Believe in him, lean on him know that he is there a few of us already know that there is power in prayer Amen!!!

The Ride

If life was a car, how far could you go when it doesn't use gas
it.
Moves by the message from God and how you perceive it
you'll move fast or slow.

When you fill up on Sunday to be blessed on Monday, you
wonder how the rest of your week will go, because the day is
not promised to anyone thus far don't you know.

The direction you take may bring you to a dead end. If you
don't have our lord god as your savior and friend. Many have
been blessed and some put to the test. His mercy and his
grace will allow you to face any conditions you endure on this
ride. Because only time will tell if the weather changes that'll
cause you to slip and slide.

The ride of life has no breaks, you'll make many moves with
lots of mistakes. Giving honor to God with plenty of praise
will get you amped up and on your way.

The ride of life can be deadly or sweet, the ride of life can
sweep you off your feet. Jesus take the wheel, take a hold of
our mind, mend it and heal it with the test of time. Driving
this metal weapon is not the same as the armor of God, this 4
wheeled contraption can take us by storm; end your life and
leave many torn.

So, the next time you endure the ride, make sure you put
God 1st each and every time. Have an open mind keep goo
by your side, you'll never know if this drive is your last ride.

NO MORE

Dark days cold nights. The whistling of the wind as it blows at night. The glimpse of sunshine, the smell of the rain. The sound of thunder and the feeling of pain.
NO MORE
The smell of fresh cut grass. The shimmering of the morning dew. The sound of laughter, a cry for attention, the warmth of your body let's not forget the beating heart too.
NO MORE
The thoughts of the wise, the jokes from being silly and cool. The tender feeling of knowing someone cares for you. The wet feel of water the cold feeling of snow.
NO MORE
The wicked ways of the world. The sadden stories we hear. The presence of a loved one near and dear. The sighs and sheds of tears, the hurting feeling of being alone full of fear.
NO MORE
The clear blue sky, the shade beneath a tree. The memories of you and me forever will-·soar. Even if I am.
NO MORE

In The Mist of The Rain:

In the mist of the rain, we all complain.
In the mist of the rain, we hide our pain.
In the mist of the rain the drops can hide our tears.
In the mist of the rain the storm rises our fears.
When it rains it pours yet a cool breeze soars and the rain
goes deep into the earth to nourish the ground in which we
must all be laid down.

REMEMBER ME

Full of life and hope, wondering if the next person I meet will
not be a joke
REMEMBER ME
When I had to sacrifice and all that I had so you could smile
REMEMBER ME
The days-I was sad with no one to talk or to call
REMEMBER ME
Today as I lean on God to help me see a better me and have
a clean heart
REMEMBER ME
When I complete my journey as his faithful servant, and I do
my part

REMEMBER ME
Smiling, dancing, walking, talking, and giving you all of me
and my woes
REMEMBER ME
When I am no more of this earth, keeping images of my life
even if it was my worst
REMEMBER ME
As I put Jesus Christ first our Lord and Savior whom has
planned this from my birth

A Special Delivery

When every knock at your door, brings trouble your way. When every call you answer makes you want to scream and say. Lord, I need you today, I need to find my way. You walk about with lots on your mind, but clearly this is your normal time after time.

You're on the way to work, and you replay all the events that caused you to hurt. Your mind is not focused, and your spirit is tainted, all this negative energy came from the previous statement. Who do you vent to; do you know if they really care. However, in your mind sometimes out loud you swear. Because the person you called is not there, to calm you down to give you peace. When you really need to call on God pray and release.

As the day goes on, you feel that everything you do will not be completed. Because you let all your, woos cause you to feel defeated. But if you have faith and believe in the almighty king you can hear a melody in your mind that your heart will sing. Acknowledge our lord when you experience turmoil in your life, you need to realize there is passion after the pain it's called a spiritual gain. All because Jesus Christ gave his life, you do not need to call on man or a vice.

A special delivery arrives just on time. Because we serve an honest god, he can ease your mind. A special delivery will give you hope no need to worry, you just hold on it's not the end of the rope. When the tears stop, and your anxiety subsides. God will turn your pain into passion by and by. Just stay on track a special delivery is on its way. God hears your cry hallowed be thy name. A special delivery is awaiting, for each of you. Remember God can make a way. Don't just put his power on a shelf all you need to do is start believing in yourself.

Don't let today or tomorrow slow you down. Keep on pressing through. A special delivery is on the way to help pull you through.

Christ-must!!!

The most wonderful time of the year brings good tides and cheer. With presents and love from family far and near. Truly, you know that a good saint will show the meaning of Christmas and how the story goes. Jesus of Nazareth was born and celebrated, on the 25th of December the north star is a way to guide us so that we remember.

To feel an abundance of cheer. Christ - must be in your view not your rear. His words and teachings can help you start a new and to live without fear. It has been said that Jesus was conceived and crucified on the same date in different years. Therefore, Christmas is celebrated near the end of the year. But Christ - must be celebrated throughout the year regardless of the date. Especially if you believe in God and have faith.

Christ- must know your true heart. You should pray that he lights a way for you through the dark. The Christmas tree has branches that represent Christ crown of thorns on the crucifixion. When we think of Christmas we forget to mention. The tree of life with lights topped by a star, symbolizes the resurrection of Jesus Christ with his bruises and his scar.

We celebrate with gifts under the tree. Please keep in mind Jesus' salvation can set you free. The greatest gift to man that is known is life, honor our lord and savior remember what he sacrificed. Be happy, be merry, remember we all have a cross to carry. Be mindful, be meek, Christ-must know you walk with him on the same beat.

Christ-must live in you for all your days, Christ-must hear your voice as you speak out loud and pray. Blessings on blessings to all of you with cheer, have a merry Christmas and a happy new year.

Amen!!

When Your Vice Controls You

What do you do that pleases you? Can you stop it, or does it linger for a few? There is a monkey on your back. How far will you carry him, and will you take a backpack and a snack? You do understand that the man with the plan "God" has carried you through and through. But you don't pray, and your praying power is depleted because you and the monkey together are so conceited. You forgot how to pray but you say you do daily. But there is this monkey that makes you forget and feel amazing, but in reality, you look crazy.

You have no power to pray you just forfeit it. But yes sir, yes ma'am you need it. Stop feeding this monkey and let God feed you the word. He has a full course meal; it is the discernment of the spirt you should be concerned. Take a look in the mirror who do you see? Does this image represent something godly?

When your vice controls you. Your soul is tarnished, I pray that you have people around you to get you back varnished. Shine for the lord. Have thanksgiving in your heart. Break free of this monkey because he really wants to tear you apart. Drink from the fountain of living waters (Jeremiah 2:11-13) you should be thirsty or so it seems.

Revise this life, let go of the vice. Think about it, when you listen to a spiritual song you feel oh so warm and yet you move about like bees in a swarm. Aimlessly looking for a moment to take. Please believe in God he makes no mistakes.

Display what you love, listen to the heavens above. Be proud of what you do. Know that our lord god can bring prosperity to you. Trust in him, lean on him, and win with him. Remember that monkey is not on your level, get rid of him, before you sink and swim.

The Man I See

I do not want to go to school today. The kids make fun of me they laugh, and they say, who are you, go away there-is no room for you to come and play. I do not want to go home after school my family is mean and cruel. I have to fake a smile to pretend that I am not hurt, I have to sleep in my pants and my shirts.

I overheard a group of kids talking about Jesus Christ. So, I walked toward their direction because I wanted to hear more about his life. But one of the mean kids meet me with a heavy blow a powerful strike. I saw stars while others watched and stood in sight.

There is no one that will listen, no one that will help, when I go home bruised, I will still see the end of a belt. Every day I struggle to get up and stay positive even when I feel I do not want to live. Someone please show me how to love and how to have strong will.

I had the chance to see a man, but I am certain I was the only one that could see. He said his name was Jesus Christ come follow me. I reached out my hand and I felt so overjoyed. All the bruises and blemishes were removed, and I did not feel avoid.

I wonder if my parents ever loved me, I wonder if the kids actually got to know me how would my life be. The man I met that only I could see, showed me more love and how great my life could be.

Now that I have found my inner strength, I can hold my head up and smile proud because I am loved I am god's beautiful child. I have meaning, I have faith, and I will not let others get in my way for goodness sake.

Amen!!!

God's will

How do you make it through your day? Especially if you do not kneel and pray. When do you start to believe in the will of God, because all that you do seems a bit odd, while you run around with a wicked squad.

Are you aware of the 4 steps to follow god's will? They are very sound and just, following this path you still can thrive and thrust, just keep your faith in him and trust.

You need to 1st believe in Jesus Christ, he is love and the light. 2nd you need to abstain from sexual sin and love the skin you're in. 3rd you should give thanks in everything and honor thy king, to gain your wings. 4th you should submit in doing right even if you suffer from it all day and or all night.

God's will can cover you, even with all your inabilities to be good he will cover you with his feathers till you are safe even if you feel misunderstood.

How do you make it through your day? You should start out by thanking Jesus, just open your mouth and say today god's will shall be done even if I cannot see the end results. Noah built an ark and Jesus walked up to a boat. God's will. 4 steps to follow open your mind, no need to be shallow or hollow.

Amen!!!

The Face You See

Everyone has a distinctive look. Yet, we all are created in the likes of his image, and to know him you need to pray and read the book. Some faces you see comes with a mystery and a story to unfold. But if you read the scripture and some of the scrolls. The face you cannot see is the true one in control. When you see someone smile you believe that they are happy and overjoyed and when you see someone frown you believe that they are sad and or annoyed.

The power of God can change your image and reposition your face. His love and anointing can cover you with his grace. When you display a look that does not fit the lifestyle you show. It is not hard to see that any moment you will reap what you sow. The face you see could easily be someone with a pure heart. But some faces you see can be beautiful and deadly and truly want to rip you apart.

The face you cannot see is God and he is always there from the start. So, when you close your eyes and hide your face you are blocking blessings from God the man you cannot trace. But if you open your eyes and except your rightful place and have just a little faith. You can hold your head up high and have certainty that God will show mercy and reposition your face.

The face you see may come with scars and marks that does not mean you should fear. Jesus Christ had scars and was wounded by a spear and yet his apostles went out to spread the word of the newborn faith. So, the face you see may be beautiful with a sinister smile lurking to see how you react. However, in fact the face you cannot see will protect thee, if your belief is small as a mustard seed.

The face you may not see comes with all authority you should want to be a disciple and be baptised.in the name of the father, the son, and the holy spirit. The face you see in the mirror should believe in God and also be considerate as well as deliberate.

Amen!!!

Stone bed and soft pages

Scritta paper is thin and durable it is made of wood pulp, containing.
Cotton or linen fibers. Some powerful words have been written in the scrolls and this paper has many messages untold. It holds basic information before leaving earth better known as the bible it speaks of many things including Jesus death and birth.

There are stories of a child in a manger, surrounded by farm animals, shepherds and wise men. Some travelled into Bethlehem to find the baby the angels told them about. He is the living word we read on soft pages; he is what life and love is about.

As a baby, he was laid on a stone bed and yet his life was depicted on soft pages. His bed was not made of wood as we have seen in nativity sets over the ages. Later, he was placed in a tomb sealed off with a large stone after they crucified him and did him wrong.

Later he rose with all power displaying the wounds from man. He has risen thank you father god - we know that man does not understand. He died for our sins, he shed blood 7 times for our salvation. When a soldier noticed he was already dead he still pierced his side causing some damnation.

Although this soldier had an eye issue at that time. The blood and water that fell from Jesus healed this man and yet this battle still has not been won. But he did acknowledge that this man is truly god's son.

In conclusion, you may start out on a stone bed, be crucified, and mocked. You may even be wounded and scared by a flock, just know that soft pages will guide you through it's the bible that will carry you. Believe in his power, believe in his name a stone bed and soft pages will always remain.

Amen

The Cross to Bear

How heavy is your burden? What trials do you have to deal with? When there are storms and battles in your life, with no fulfillment.
A spiritual feeling of happiness and satisfaction living for Christ, is the fulfillment we all need in our life. To be a part of god's works and beliefs, we need to understand the main purpose of his promise to never leave us and keep us safe from harm.

No need to be evil and falsify your charm. God is the Almighty he will bear arms. Psalm 91 will explain that you are safe from harm.
Giving God the glory and walking your path, will bring you closer to our lord with no questions asked. You will experience a wicked vibe from a person who does not walk in your stride.

Beware of a bad spirit that looks like a friend because they are everywhere, Jesus had two men alongside of him walking with his cross to bear. They also hung high up in the air. One was called a good thief and the other unrepentant, this is to let you know that we all need to repent.

The cross to bear is a journey you must take on your own. When God looks upon you while sitting on his throne. He shines a light so precious and true. When people see the god in you, they will help you carry your cross just like Simon of Cyrene did with Jesus who paid the cost. Many followed but one came through this cross weighed 165 pounds to carry it alone how would you? This should be enough to make you want to be a part of the gospel and teach more than just a few. The cross to bear, sometimes is not fair, but let the world see the god in you and show that you care.

Amen!!

I Know Him for Myself

As soon as I wake up, i thank the lord for allowing me to see this day. However, my entire day - yesterday was full of incidents that could have easily broken me. But I know God kept me from all unsettling issues. Even though i cried like a baby and needed lots of tissue.

The weight of this old wretched world can fall like a ton of bricks. But I know him for myself, so these issues are already fixed. God kept me and promised me a new day. As long as I open my mind, my heart, and my mouth to confess, pray and say: thank you lord god for carrying me come what may.

I know him for myself, and my god will make a way. The future of tomorrow could most definitely come with sorrow; you do understand that this earthly time is borrowed. Do you know Jesus Christ? He. should be the head of your life. Because if you are sitting around on your tail, there is no room to excel, you just fester and fail.

I know him for myself. He gave me a reason to place my issues on a shelf. It is called faith, forward all issues to heaven. Wooo!!! My God is real, and i know him for myself his love yes!!! I feel. I cannot complain because every day is new. I know him for myself, but what about you?

Amen!!!

A Box and A Shell

Living life is hard especially if you have not confessed your love for God. Life means living when you believe in the lord having faith is thanksgiving, this should not be ignored. You are a gift, a miracle, a precious creation, give your life to the lord for salvation. Understand his power believe in his name. Please do not fill your life full of shame.

Hard times and troubling situations can make your life a living hell. Give yourself to the lord before you end up in a box and a be a shell. The body you live in is just a human vessel; it is not ever lasting the bible says so. A box and a shell is not where you will dwell, especially if you give your life to our lord oh what stories they will tell.

God gave you a soul and a spirit. Be patient and listen wait on the lord and you will hear it. When he speaks to you his message will make sense. Pick a side you need to stop straddling the fence. A box is not how you came into this world, a shell is not you; but your soul and your spirit still lives on in a few.

Make a joyful noise, give God the highest praise, before you end up in a box and a shell for the rest of your days. Because with God in your life you will live on. Give yourself away and be reborn. His mansion awaits for you because, by his mercy, and by his grace if you love him this box and this shell is not your final resting place.

Amen

On My Way to Heaven

On my way to heaven, it will be a beautiful show. Full of laughter and love with a marching band, spiritual songs, and a conductor we all know. Of course, theft will be tears and sorrow, but this trip will not be repeated after tomorrow. So, dry your face because I had a good race I no longer dwell here in this place.

On my way to heaven, i may not get to see you before I go. Please keep in mind my god allowed me enough time here to reap what I sow. My journey may have not been what you expected. But I gave my life to the lord, with his armor I am protected.

On my way to heaven, my voice will be loud and clear, hollering Jesus Christ my lord and savior is here. I won't put up a fight I will not fuss, I'll hold on to his hand because it's in God I trust. On my way to heaven, it will be a joyful day, my family and friends will gather around with memories, and pray with lots to say.

I wasn't ready to go or I would have told you so. I am listening to my lord and I heard him say, that he will come back for all his children one day. You should use this heavenly message to get prayed up and be ready for your storm. You die once but live every day. Give your life to Jesus Christ and you are re-born. Put your adventures in order, remove all your devilish ways, to start your journey.
To heaven you need to knell and pray.

On my way to heaven, I will know that my mission is complete. I gave God the Glory while I was here standing on my two feet. On my way to heaven my shell will be laid to rest, all while I rejoice Father God, I love you; you are the best. You gave me life, instilled in me a clean heart. I only wish that I had known how to love you more from the very start.

On my way to heaven, hallowed be thy name. He is an awesome god; I hope you feel the same. On your journey to heaven, I hope you remember that special day. That the angles in heaven whispered in my ear and signed my name.

A Poor Black Woman with A Rich Heart

Everyone has a story, so where do I begin. Everyone has a
voice to be heard and most of us live in sin. Keeping up with
the joneses is what some people do. I am not only speaking
of me, but i am also talking about you. Coming up in a world
of lies and deceit, never praying or paying attention to those
that creep.

There are days that you worry and scurry around. Waiting for
a miracle to happen all while you wear a frown. You wonder
how you will fend for yourself and make a difference. But you
cannot seem to stop straddling the fence with repetition.
When there is nothing, you see that will enhance your sight, it
gets harder to close your eyes and sleep at night.

Poverty comes in many forms. Wealth comes with many
storms. Life is nothing if you are not re-born. Thanking the
lord above, for giving me reason to be.
Because when it's dark and I cannot see you always make a
way for me. I may be.
Poor, I am most definitely black, I am not rich, and my heart
sometimes hits the floor. But I have faith in our lord
forevermore.

A poor black woman with a rich heart is where I will start. I have to believe in myself before others tear me apart. I look to the heavens; i move through the valley and hills because moving my mountains is very real. A poor black woman with a rich heart may be how you see me. A black woman with a heart is how God created me. Because my heart is rich full of God's glory. I am a black woman but that's not all to my story. Even though I may not have a lot to give but with God I can soar. So, when I look at others living in sin, without God you cannot win. You see my friend, that to me is poor.

Amen!!!

A Letter to My Lord

Dear Lord, what shall I do, I have many things that flow through my mind at the same time. I have visions, thoughts, and the sound of music to drown out my faults. I want to be made whole and solid as a rock. Dear lord, I've seen many things that have put me in shock. Not knowing what to say to you, because sometimes my thoughts are blocked.

Dear Lord, what shall I do, I am lost. I feel I have no were to turn, but my Lord only you can stop this crash and burn. Hold me Lord caress and ease my mind. Satan is busy and he causes me to waist precious time. But it is to you my precious Lord I turn too, then man gets in the way of me starting a new.

Dear Lord, what shall I do, when all the chips are down and there is nothing, I can say or do. My Lord and Savior I need your favor. Bring me out of the depts of sin, my lord, with you I know I will win. My words are mighty, my heart is true. I believe in your power, so I give myself to you. Cleans me oh Lord help me begin a new, when others have forsaken me and I can't stand at the pew.

Father God, I write this letter because i come to you bearing my soul. You have been good to me when this world has treated me cold. Dear lord, what shall I do when I feel like this - maybe I'll just write a letter to you my lord with high hopes, love and my wish. Then seal it with a kiss dear lord.

Amen!!!

When You Serve a Different Purpose

Life is precious, right from the start. One will never know what good deeds you will do, especially from the heart. You are born fresh as the mornings dew, did you know that the original bible was written in Hebrew. Hebrew also means pass over; it signifies transition. Jesus died then rose up on the 3rd day the bible has mentioned.

Many things rise up from the ground to nourish our internal being. However, each of these things have different meanings. Trees and grass grow from the same ground. Yet serve a different purpose one is green one is brown. Depending on the season those colors will change, just like a broken relationship, nothing remains the same.

Human life and animal life both come from the womb, but only one gets carried at the end of life to the tomb. A pencil and a pen can be shaped the same, one is permanent, and one can be erased away. When you allow God to guide your way, you gain the spiritual vision of sight he will even bless your hearing even while you sleep at night.

When you serve a different purpose, you will soon come to know that somethings and some people around you will not grow and cannot go. Jesus left behind all the people who believed in his gospel. Those that didn't believe wondered around dark with deep depression and plague or needed a hospital.

When you serve a different purpose hallelujah praise the lord. Surround yourself with people on your same accord. Just because you have life doesn't mean you have purpose. But if you purposely love your life and Jesus Christ you will learn to serve and obey our lord.

Amen!!!

Doing What You Want Ignoring God's Will

When you find yourself getting involved with others life - you quickly remember that you forgot why you truly need to seek Jesus Christ. A man of God will always know that you will reap what you sow. But as long as Jesus Christ is in your life you can spiritually grow.

If you keep listening to your surroundings, and doing what you want you'll soon find that there is a judas amongst you ready to defy or have some damage done, this could be anyone. But if you believe in our lord, you will feel free, he will protect. You and bring prosperity to your life. You can wake up to see all his work from the trees to the birds and the bees.

Stop doing it your way. Let Jesus take the wheel for your infamous thrill, give yourself a way to our god and his Favor you will feel. Because when you do what you want ignoring God's will. Your next steps may be slow, you might not be able to move and most definitely not grow.

Be blessed, with no stress. Start following God and you will see that you can rest. Conduct your home as if was a tabernacle break free of the sinful chains and shackles. Remember if you keep doing what you want and ignoring gods will, you will keep living the same unrighteous life hour after hour. Because with no prayer there is no power. Amen!!!

It's A Lovely Day

Walking down the street. Listening to the pavement as it connects with your feet. Engulfing a cool breath of air with a smile on your face as if you did not have a care. This is how you will feel when your full of the godspill (gospel) your ears will hear hummingbirds sing a spiritual song. It's a lovely day to give God praise, it only takes a second to pray. When our lord has kept you through the night. Rejoice and embrace the mornings sunlight with a song. "Something about the name of Jesus" oh my Lord today I will try to-do no wrong.

It's a lovely day, no time for the walk of shame. Walk in Jesus footsteps he will guide your way. Come on to me, my father's house has many rooms that will comfort you at the end of your earthly days. He loves you unconditionally, he listens to you pray. When you weep and feel lost just know that i am there. Be kind and mindful please be peaceful and do not swear.

It's a lovely day that the lord has made ooooh... Chile....
Things are   .,
Gonna get easier. Ooooh chile   it's a lovely day so let today be
Much brighter. When the sun rays shine upon your face, you still have time to receive his mercy and his grace.

It's a lovely day god has carried you through, this is a lovely day your blessings are on the way. Believe in our god there is nothing he cannot do. You should love this day and every day that the lord wakes you up to.

The Man in My Life

The man in my life, you cannot see. Has shown me visions of something so heavenly. A vision so pure and promising as the journeys involving the Jordan river. This vision will be a part of me to remember.

My life without this man, had its days. But most of them days I did nothing worthy, not even kneel and pray. I just did my own thing and went about my way. Oh, but once I heard that door slam and seen another one open. My body went into a very deep convulsion.

The man in my life I thought was a dream. Was standing there with seven beautiful angels with wings. Each of them had a message and a gift, which made me want to leave behind the days when I did nothing but drift.

My days and nights have changed. Some may look at me strange or in disarray. But the man in my life said come unto me, you no longer need to astray. My heavenly father heard your cry every single day.

The man in my life brings a smile to my face. He comforts me and walks with me at a steady pace. I will not turn and look back, I will not belittle mankind, nor will I look down at your lifestyle or try to rewind.

My life with this man now has purpose. I no longer want to be an animal or a clown in the world's greatest circus. The man in my life has a plan for me. He has shown me how to love and let go, to forgive, and to stay humble. Even when others whisper and mumble and yet they still stumble.

But most important He allowed me to hear His word and believe in my faith. Anyone with faith and believes in his word can come follow me today. So put your best foot forward and come this way, our Lord awaits you every single day.

Amen!!!

Nothing But the Blood

When the Lord blesses, me I feel free. He gives me discernment of the spirit yes; a humble servant like me. He showed the believers that his power is so divine. At the wedding of St. John, the evangelist and Mary Magdalen he turned water into wine.

He also spoke of moments when man would lose his faith. He endured many bruises and scars for our sins, he did not bear arms or go against his kin. He wore a crown of thorns long before you and I were born, and yet as of this day his anointing is real.

He died and rose up; soon to the world his powers were revealed. I am the alpha and the omega. Come unto me and receive favor. Many followed, many fled, some of his words lingered in their heads. To a few he was just a man. To the spiritual hearts he had the master's plan.
Love thy neighbor, give more than you receive. Acknowledge I am your lord and for you I will bleed. If you believe in my father, you shall meet him through me. All I ask is that you deny yourself and abstain from the sins of the flesh.

Live each day for God. Be a living sacrifice. He will cover you with his armor, Jesus already paid the price. Same as he protected Noah, his family and two of every living thing of male and female specimen. Noah followed god's command to build an ark. Because he believed in god's word to be protected from the flood.

This serves as proof of his love. So, what can wash away your sin and make you whole again. It's not man or your best bud. If you believe in Jesus, then you know it's nothing but the blood.

Amen!!!

Taking Care of The Man of The House

When God had a plan to create man from dry land. He designed him in the likes of his image, to do his work spiritually in the moral nature. He is our father, our Lord, our creator, our Savior.

Moses was called to build god's tabernacle, Noah was called to build god's ark, and our pastor has been called to lead St. Mark. Peter was called to build Jesus a church, to encourage saints to unite in righteousness. Although he denied Jesus and he was a witness to his rebirth.

Taking care of the man of the house has many levels. Having a solid foundation and a strong congregation helps to defeat the enemy also known as the devil. When the man of the house calls upon you. There should be no hesitation, you should rejoice in manifestation. Because we know that in all living things god works for the greater good, but sometimes his works and messages are misunderstood.

Gods plan lives in all of us. As we walk into the house of our supreme being make a loud joyful noise praise and sing. Do not be afraid to scream and shout, open your eyes, your ears, and your mouth. Love the Lord and keep taking care of the man of the house.

Amen!!!

Wonder Woman

People may wonder why God gave his only son as sacrifice, people may wonder how others live their righteous or unholy life. Some people wonder about a woman in many ways, or it could even be a man now a days. All the while they turn away from gods unchanging hand, never kneel and pray. A man is known to be powerful on his own as it seems.

But a wonder woman by His side is exactly what he needs. A wonder woman 'like Mary Magdalene who had issues but was loyal and walked with Jesus to show her faith, she was full of 7 demons but healed by the Lord's grace. A wonder woman so bold and right on queue, she was there for Jesus' crucifixion and his resurrection, this is true. She was one of the few women disciples of Jesus Christ and she followed him through and through. Even wonder men Peter, James and John also walked with him too. Just like Mary, a wonder woman that sounds like me it can even be you. She hailed from a small town near Galilee, I am from a small city F.L.I.N.T. people wonder about the woman I am. I know I am a woman that will make you wonder, but God my creator gave me a gift to move peoples soul like the sound of thunder. This is my journey to walk with Jesus; yes, I have history, yes, I have a past, but that will not stop me from learning to be whole with God - because that feeling will forever last. I am a woman full of wonder, who will not forsake thee, even when the odds are against me. Praising my lord for the things I have and the things I cannot see. Honoring his holly name, and to keep following the path he created for me. This is my testimony, my destiny.

History Of Our Race

Our skin is dark and sometimes light, we have many obstacles to deal with and fight. We have come a long way, and the struggle is real. As we hold on to God, his love we can feel.

God created Adam to do his work and carry out his mission. He then created eve from Adam's rib as the bible has mentioned. The history of our race begins in the book of genesis, as it speaks of the dark and the light.

We all know that every race has some history. February is a month chosen to celebrate African American history. But we can celebrate our race all year long and praising god with spiritual songs.

We have 28 days to honor our race, 360 days holding on to God for mercy and grace. Don't let one month of celebrating bring you joy about your kin. Keep God in your life, remembering his sacrifice and live without sin.

The history of our race is seen upon our face. Today and every day is a day that God, has made let us be glad and rejoice in it. Because it doesn't matter if you are light or dark keep the faith and have God in your heart.

A Vision in Time

A vision in time is so divine no need to be quiet as a mouse, raise your voice and bring down the house when you are alone or with your spouse. God gives you wisdom to see that all things are connected for the greater good. This is also a reason why he is so misunderstood. Man does not have the knowledge, if you could ask eve. Man is full of shame so please believe that God is all you need.

Open your mind feel with your heart. Jesus bleeds to give you a new start. A vision in time does not stand still. You will not be able to rewind it because a vision in time is a mental thrill that has more power than you know, this is why you will reap what you sow. A vision in time can cause you to stop, listen, and stand still. Or it can spin you around like a hamster wheel.

A vision in time can show the present or the past. God has a vision in time, if you believe in him that vision will last. Listen between the seconds as the clock ticks away. Making a clicking noise before the dawn of the new day. You begin to notice the sounds of the night, sometimes afraid to close your eyes because without God your thoughts can be an awful fright.

A vision in time will make you laugh or cry. A vision in time can make you wonder why, was this world created for you and I. A vision in time should keep you focused because life is full of tricks - hocus pocus, pray for Favor because God is the Almighty, the alpha and the

Omega. To endure this vision god has to save ya. Read king James

Version of genesis 15, 1 Samuel 3, Daniel 7-12, acts 9, Cornelius and
Peter both in acts 10. With a vision in time god's people will surely win.

African American

As we celebrate our history. There are many facts that remind us of who we are. Carter g. Woodson made it possible for us as African Americans to be recognized and acknowledged for accomplishments in 1926. The month of February was chosen because Abraham Lincoln and Frederick Douglas were born in that month. By 1976 President Gerald R. Ford reserved the month as a holiday.

When goo created Adam and eve there is no mention of their skin. We know them as the mother and father of all humans which makes us all kin and God's grace still covers us even when we sin. To know your true self, you must trust in God, he will make a way even if you are flawed.

Look around, see the face of your brothers and sisters. We all dwell in the same land holding on to God's unchanging hand. As an African American we celebrate this month with honor for those who have paved the way. So, keep praising God for heaven's sake, he is the reason we rise and wake every day.

12 months equal 1 year. So, lets celebrate and give God cheer for creating us in his image, we should worship him and not live in fear. There is no comparison to be African American if God is in your life. February is just one month so, celebrate your African American history all of your life giving honor to those who paid the price.

Amen!!!

Forevermore

Love a powerful word. L-lasting, o-omnipotence, v-valiant, E-empowered
That's what love means to me forevermore I'll give God the honor. Love can be bold, and love can be true forevermore father god I love you. I did not know how to show the love in me no one taught me about thee. I tried to understand in my mind, but my thoughts were blurry.

Who was the man my grandmother spoke of many times before she also said she loved him forevermore. I never seen him nor heard his voice. However, she would sing, smile, and rejoice. Sometimes I was afraid to ask, gram who is this man that causes you to act this way. She said chile his name is Jesus you need to learn to kneel and pray.

I thought she was crazy and lost her mind. My grandfather's name was johnnie I thought she was getting out of line. I never seen her leave the house to attend church. I never seen her buy fancy hats or dresses at any store and yet she would still say she loved this man forevermore.

He never ate dinner with us, but she would praise his name. She would thank him for our meals and all that we had. Even though some days when there was not much food and she looked very sad.
I will always remember those days forevermore. Especially when I see her kneel on the floor. She cried out lord I need thee, the love I hold in my heart will always be.

Forevermore my life has changed. My grandmother is no longer here but as she did, I did for my family, and I learned to kneel and pray. Forevermore the love inside of me will soar. I'll teach my children and grandchildren how to love even when I am no more.

Amen!!!

Break Every Chain

Sunday is the beginning and the last day of the week. Sunday should be everyday if its god you seek. Far too many times we let problems lock us down. Then you praise one day a week and other days you wear a frown. Then you call on your pastor, but he needs prayer too. You want him to pray to God to heal you and carry you through. But have you given any thought that he has things going on as well.

All the while you are crying and bringing him all your - hell -0 "his voicemail picks up; this is pastor Kevin Thompson leave a message at the beep" now you are in disbelief that he didn't answer. So, you say "I'm not leaving a message, I want my. Blessings I'll call back or see him at church after. But you haven't attended service in a long time, now you think his sermon is about you and you try to put a damper on his shine. Although you are not reading your bible nor walking in the spirit. You holler thank you Jesus so loud that everyone can hear it.

Why do you do this? God's love is free will. Insert yourself stay calm and chill. Let God's love flow like rain. Let it move fast through you like a freight train. Give him the glory and tell your story on how to break every chain. Our pastor is still a man, he experience's joy and pain. Get to know the lord for yourself, because attending church on Sunday's refreshes your soul so you don't feel insane. But you should be spiritually motivated every day and not let it be the same. God's people, it is time to break every chain.

Outside Of Myself

Hello, how are you, can you hear me? What can I do to help? What· do you mean? I am ok, don't I look that way? I smile to hide the hurt,
Sometimes I wish I was buried in the dirt. I move with ease, and I try very hard to please anyone, but somehow, I get teased. My mind is full of words, but I don't feel heard. I stare into the sky because I wonder why, I want to die. When I look around all I want is to be in the ground.

No one loves me, unless the bruises are love taps, I've been beaten so many times I feel trapped. I'm in a room full of people and yet I feel alone, I even have scars and a few broken bones. I try to fit in, I wish I had a twin, I walk around un-assure, I hide behind corners & live in sin, but my heart is pure.

Goodbye, I thought you could help, this is what I mean, I am outside of myself. When I cry, I feel relieved, I prayed to God on bended knee. Save me lord from myself I know longer know my worth, I feel, I have no value here on earth. I tried to love myself and keep an open mind, but I have nothing else to give at this time.
Forgive me family and friends for thinking of committing a sin, this is a battle I cannot win
Can not win. If I put a picture of me on your shelf, life isn't for me anymore I am outside of myself.

Hour Of Power

A room full of strangers, with stories to tell. A room full of strangers who have been through some hell. A room full of strangers eating food together with a wonderful smell. Who had this idea? How could this be? Well, sit with us and have a talk with Mrs. Shirley.

A wonderful woman full of gods power, sometimes are time with her runs over an hour. However, the relief we gain holds us together because we thought we were insane. Hour of power we talk about life. We even praise Jesus' name.

A room full of believers, a room full of achievers, a room full of love and God is the receiver. St. Mark outreach center is where it's at. No need to be a member just come, sit, and chat. You also do not need to speak. Just listen till the end, you might discover yourself and gain a new friend.

We all have our woes; it is time to let the miracles begin. So, when you are feeling down, and it feels like no one cares. On Tuesdays come to hour of power we will be waiting there.

The doors are open, come visit for a few. God is also present there, so come sit and enjoy our crew. Elder Naphier and Deacon Davis created this for you, hour of power can heal and reset you from feeling sour. Hour of power come witness God's love showers.

Amen!!!

Separated From Your Spirit

We are all created in the image of God. So, we are filled with the holy spirit, a gift from the man in charge. When the holy spirit has caressed you - your mind is open for the serpent to test you. Sometimes you pray, sometimes you fight in your inner spirit, even when others cannot hear it or see it in plain sight.

Separated from your spirit has its own life. Because one part of you ain't living right. While the other half is barley holding on with the belief in Jesus Christ, and then Satan says come on. Your spirit is tainted, your tears we see, however, when was the last time you were on bended knee asking God to forgive thee?

When the world was dark, He said let there be light. He created the human soul so loving and so bright. He also gave the devil permission to test your faith, steal, kill and torture. Waiting to see if you love God enough to come to the alter.

Separated from your spirit will give you false hope. People look at you and know this maybe the end of your rope. Still not sure how you are making it and how do you cope? When you are separated from your spirit you do not have God's yoke. The devil steps in and now you are provoked.

To believe in God, you need to be in the spirit. Pull it all back together rejoice and adhere it. Separated from your spirit can be repaired. Keep giving God the glory there is no one that can compare.

Ask yourself, be honest, be true. Are you separated from the spirit? Remember God see's the real you.

Amen!!!

Beautiful Blessings

Holidays are fun and holidays bring cheer. As we entertain our families, far and near let's prepare for the new year.

We see beautiful blessings with lots of smiles if you're in town or driving for miles.

Children are eager to play with all the new things they have got. If you are-naughty you get coal in your sock.

Everyone brings gifts to exchange, sometimes a dish that gets passed, hopefully no one complains, and it gets eaten really fast.

Beautiful blessings are being with loved ones and friends. Grandma makes pies and rolls the dough with a wooden pin.

When the adults get together, they sing songs of long ago, and when Uncle Kevin hits high notes we all holler oh noooooo.

The smell of cookies, fruit, and pies is a beautiful blessing itself. Even the little babies try to reach up high and pull them off the shelf.

Happy holidays may your blessings be beautiful. May your new year be just as fruitful.

Beautiful blessings to all of you with cheer. Merry Christmas and happy new year.

I Am Hungry

I am hungry lord my belly makes a gurgling sound that I feel in my feet. I fell to the floor tonight on bended knee, lord god help me, I am so hungry. I went about my day, and I continued to pray until my body was weak. I am hungry my lord. My stomach is touching my back, I haven't eaten in a week.

To God be the glory it is the knowledge of the word I seek. Feed me oh lord, I will not forsake thee. Give me strength to endure these days without a meal, I have made some mistakes along the way but by his stripes I am healed.

The older I get. Life gets rougher, I do not know if the next meal I have will be my last supper. But my faith and your word will keep me knowledgeable and fed, I have learned to make better decisions in my life as I break bread.

Although, I am hungry within my body father god, I am hungry for you this is true. You gave me this life I messed up my own stew. Giving too much and taking too little. Now I belong to a church that is now my hospital. I am hungry my lord, so hungry I cannot sleep. Trying to figure my next mission in this world to complete.

There is a song in my heart, and joy in my spirit. Father my stomach is growling so loud I know that you can hear it. At the end of the day, I still will call on you and pray. Giving honor to you for all the things you have done and will do for me. Hallelujah, thank you Jesus I will kneel down and pray even when I am hungry.

The Space In Between

Have you ever felt held down and nailed up? Do you remember what happened in your life between the ages of 12 and 30? All the while walking on solid ground, is your foundation sturdy? When you turned 18 do you understand the space in between the life of Jesus from a boy to a man is the same time frame when most of us at that age don't even have a plan.

It makes you wonder. How is this so, the space in between our own lives some of us don't even know. Life can be like a freight train, full of things to deliver and moving very fast. Causing friction on the tracks full steam ahead with a very loud blast. It only goes forward it cannot go in reverse. So, get to know God the creator of our universe.

God can guide you on this journey of life. God can fill the space in between but there will be some sacrifices if you know what I mean. Put your house in order stop intentionally disobeying God you know He is always there but do you even care? The space in between life and death has a lot of areas that reach different depth's so to know God will keep you intact so watch your steps.

The space in between simply means. Praise God with conviction in your heart. Honor thy father thy mother, that is a great start. Have faith, let go and let God.

The Women of St. Mark Baptist Church

Have you ever seen strength? Have you ever seen faith? Well, I will say, come see the women of St. Mark. These are women that truly pray. When you walk through the doors it feels like coming home. You feel that love, you could be young or old. The women of St. Mark speak as one and move as one to guide you through. Because there is a battle our there lurking and waiting on you.

The women of St. Mark are equipped with that motherly love. This discernment of the spirit comes only from heaven above. There are also good men here too, I see the young men looking up to you. We are all in a powerful godly place. Continue to come and worship with our family we will put a smile on your face.

The women of St. Mark represent a story. One that will always give God the glory. They all are special and bring their best, you should know time and time they have been put to the test. These women don't break, they may bend, just know if you are near them, you will feel the spirit with in.

The women of St. Mark - have left their mark on me. I am humble lost soul with a mind set on a journey to galilee. Why Galilee because the scriptures say that is where Christ willed to show himself openly. A women of St. Mark should be your title, because these women were sent here straight from the bible.

Amen!!!

Epilogue

Learning About God Through Poetry

I did not always understand and there is still more to learn. Somehow the spirit moved in me and to understand my existence is all I yearn. Words have always been vibrant in my mind, but when i put pen to paper, I feel the divine. This spirit gives me a wonderful feeling of love. Because it holds me like a soft leather glove.

This is no ordinary glove you see. It is the glove on the right hand of my lord; it is he. He who gives me strength and peace. Learning about God through my poetry is my spiritual release. Everyone needs an outlet, what will you choose yours to be. I choose the alpha the omega, it is God for me.

But what is poetry - poetry is written words of life, especially when it intervenes with Jesus Christ. God communicated through prophets who related to his people with an emotional connection to see their faith. In the book of psalms, job, and proverbs the text gives us words to live by and follow. These poets are just a few that crossed my mind and came into view, look them up do not wait until tomorrow.

Learning about God through poetry has opened my mind. It is allowing me time to get my life in line. It also allows me to keep my faith because I believe in his power. That's why I do more prayer to get more power. I have learned that a little prayer gives you a little power and with no prayer there is absolutely no power.

Terralisa McBride

Made in the USA
Columbia, SC
26 September 2024

43084990R00067